Enkrateia

Josan Ranjjith C.J

INDIA • UK • USA

Paperback-979-8-89171-257-7
eBook-979-8-89171-259-1

First Published on January 2026

Published by Walnut Publication

(an imprint of Vyusta Platforms Private Limited)

www.walnutpublication.com

India

Unit# 909, 9th Floor, Wave Silver Tower, Sector-18, Noida - 201301

UK

71-75 Shelton Street, Covent Garden, London, WC2H 9JQ, UK

Distributed by

DEDICATION

For every young person who is tired of feeling weak and wants to become

The master of their own life. This is for your next version.

PREFACE

This book is about change. Not the change that just happens to you, but the change

You choose. Self-transformation means you decide to grow on purpose.

Self-mastery means you learn to guide your thoughts, your actions, your habits, step by step.

You do not need big words or big plans to begin.

You need honesty, small daily effort, and the courage to face yourself.

These are simple poems for young hearts who want to rise from confusion to clarity, from weakness to strength, from automatic life to chosen life.

Read slowly. Read again. Use them to train your mind, your heart, your will.

You are not stuck. You are under construction.

CHAPTER 1. AWAKENING: SEEING YOURSELF CLEARLY

1. The First Mirror

Self-mastery starts with a mirror inside.

Not the one on your wall, but the one in your mind that shows you your habits, your fears, your excuses, your strengths.
Look, without lying. Say, "This is where I am.

This is who I am today." You cannot change what you refuse to see.

2. The Honest List

Sit down with a pen. Make two lists. On one side,

Write: "What is helping my life?" On the other side,

Write: "What is hurting my life?" Be honest: late nights, endless scrolling,

Fake friends, food, talk, attitude, anger. This is not to hate yourself. This is

To see what must stay, what must go, for you to transform.

---

3. You Are Not Just Feelings

You feel lazy. You feel scared. You feel angry.

You feel sad. Those are feelings, not commands. You do not have to obey every feeling. Self-mastery is when you say, "I feel tired, but I will still do work." "I feel afraid, but I will still take a small step." You are not just what you feel. You are the one who chooses what to do with those feelings.

4. The Story You Tell

Listen to the story you tell yourself: "I am lazy."

"I am stupid." "I am weak." "I always mess up." Your brain believes what it hears again and again. Self-transformation starts when you change the story. Say instead: "I have lazy habits, but I can build new ones." "I don't know this yet, but I can learn." "I have been weak, but I am training my strength." You are not fixed. You are a story still being written by your own words.

_____

_____

_____

_____

_____

_____

5. The Moment You Decide

There is a moment when you get tired of your own excuses. You look at your room, your marks, your body, your mind, and you know: "I can be more than this." That quiet anger, that deep frustration,
Is not your enemy. It is a signal. It is life saying, "Wake up. Decide. Change. "Self-mastery begins the moment you say, "I choose a different path."

6. Facing Your Weak Points

Everyone has weak points. Maybe you lose control when you are angry. Maybe you cannot say no. Maybe you give up quickly. Maybe you lie to avoid trouble. Do not hide from these parts. Point at them And say, "Yes. This is my weak point. But it will not stay this way forever. I will train here the most."

_____

_____

_____

_____

_____

_____

7. You Are Not Your Past

You may have done wrong things, wasted time, hurt people, and failed again and again. Your past explains you, but it does not lock you.

Self-transformation is when you say, "I accept what I did. I accept what happened. But I do not accept that this is all I will ever be." You are allowed to become better than your history.

8. Taking Back the Remote

Sometimes it feels like other people hold the remote of your life. They press a button, you get angry. They give an opinion, you feel small. They insult you, you break. Self-mastery is taking back that remote. You may still feel hurt or upset, but you learn to pause, to breathe, to choose. "I will not give every person the power to control my mood."

_____

_____

_____

_____

_____

_____

9. The Power of "I Chose This"

When you do things without thinking, you feel weak. You scroll for hours. You eat too much. You skip work. You lie on the bed, knowing you should move. Self-mastery grows when you say, "Whatever I did, I chose it." Not to blame yourself, but to take power. If you choose it, you can choose differently next time.

10. Stop Running From Silence

Many young hearts are scared of silence. No music, no phone, no noise. Just you and your thoughts. But silence is where you hear the truth. What do you want? What are you afraid of? What are you proud of? What must you change? Self-knowledge comes when you sit quietly with yourself and listen, without running away.

11. The Two You's

Inside you there are two you's. The "easy" you wants comfort now: more sleep, more food, more scrolling, less work. The "master" you wants strength later: good health, sharp mind, peaceful heart, stable life. Every choice feeds one of them. Ask, "Which me am I feeding today?"

12. The Pain of Self-Honesty

To change, you must feel a certain pain: The pain of seeing that you have wasted time. The pain of seeing that some problems are your own fault. The pain of seeing that you knew better but still chose worse. Do not run from this pain. It is medicine. It burns, but it cleans.

13. No More Blame Game

It is easy to say: "My parents. My school. My city. My friends. My past. My bad luck." Yes, these things matter. Yes, they can hurt you. But if you give them all the blame, you also give them all the power. Self-mastery says, "My life is hard, but I still have some choices. I will use what power I have, no matter how small."

14. Your Inner Coach

Imagine there is a coach inside your mind. The bad coach says, "You are useless. You will always fail. Why even try?" Fire that coach. Hire a new one in your head, one who says, "You can do better than yesterday. You are not there yet, but keep going. One more try. One more step." Train your inner voice to speak like a real coach, not a cruel judge.

15. Catching Yourself

Self-mastery does not mean you never slip. It means you catch yourself faster. You start scrolling, then stop and say, "No. Enough." You raise your voice, then pause and say, "I am getting angry. I should calm down." You skip study again, then think, "I am repeating the old pattern. Let me change it now." Every time you catch yourself, you grow stronger.

16. The Question That Changes You

Before you act, ask, "Will this make my future self stronger or weaker?" This one question can change your whole life. Angry text? Weaker. Walking away? Stronger. Another 2 hours of videos? Weaker. One hour of study then rest? Stronger. Keep asking. Keep choosing strength.

17. Becoming Your Own Parent

Maybe you did not get the guidance you needed. Maybe no one taught you about habits, emotions, discipline, and self-respect. Self-mastery is when you decide to become your own parent. You tell yourself, "Sleep now. Study now. Eat better. Apologize. Try again." You give yourself the rules and the care you always needed.

18. Stop Waiting to "Feel Ready"

You are waiting to feel ready before you change. "I will start when I feel confident." "I will try when I feel brave." "I will work when I feel motivated." But feelings follow actions, not the other way. Confidence comes after you act while scared. Motivation comes after you start while lazy. Do not wait to feel ready. Start, and ready will come later.

_____

_____

_____

_____

_____

_____

19. The Line in the Sand

One day you must draw a line in the sand of your life. On one side: old ou—careless, weak, angry, lazy, out of control. On the other side: new you—awake, honest, disciplined, learning control. Stand on the line and say, "I may still fall back sometimes, but my face and my feet will always be turned toward the new me."

20. The Decision That Stays

A real decision is not a mood. Moods change quickly. Decisions stay even when the mood is gone. You decide to transform. You decide to master yourself. Tomorrow you may feel tired, sad, bored. But the decision remains: "I am on this path no matter how I feel today." Keep that decision like a fire you protect with both hands.

CHAPTER 2 – DISCIPLINE: TRAINING YOUR HABITS

21. Discipline Is a Gift to Yourself

Discipline is not a punishment. It is a gift you give to your future self. When you sleep on time, study daily, save money, control your temper, you are sending help to the person you will be next year, in five years, in ten. Discipline says, "I care about my future enough to make better choices today."

22. Small Routines, Big Change

You do not need a perfect schedule to change your life. You need small routines you repeat. Wake up, make your bed. Drink water. Read or study for a short time. Move your body. Sleep at a fixed time. Done once, it is nothing. Done every day, it is a new life slowly forming around you.

_____

_____

_____

_____

_____

_____

23. Train Like a Beginner

When you start new habits, do not try to be a hero. Do not say, "I will study 5 hours a day from now on," when you are used to zero. Start as a beginner. Fifteen minutes of focus. Ten push-ups. Ten pages of reading. You are building a muscle called discipline. A muscle grows bit by bit.

24. Make It Easy to Win

Self-mastery is not about making life as hard as possible. It is about making the right thing easier. Keep your books on your table, not buried. Turn off extra notifications. Charge your phone away from your bed. Lay out your clothes for a morning walk the night before. Set up your life in a way that helps you win.

25. The Two Minutes Rule

If something takes less than two minutes, do it now. Throw the trash. Reply to a simple message. Put the dish in the sink. Write the homework title. Tiny actions keep your world clean and clear. When you handle small things quickly, big things scare you less.

26. Show Up First

On many days you will not feel like doing what you planned. Do not wait for the perfect mood. Just show up. Open the book. Start the first line. Do the first push-up. Clean the first corner. Tell yourself, "I only need to begin." Often, once you start, your mind follows and the work becomes easier.

_____

_____

_____

_____

_____

_____

27. Protect Your Focus

Your focus is your strength. Every time you go from book to phone, phone to chat, chat to video, you lose it. Create islands of focus: For 25 minutes, no phone, no social media, just one task. Then rest. Then repeat. Deep work for short times beats shallow work for long times.

28. Replace, Don't Just Remove

When you try to stop a bad habit, do not only remove it. Replace it. Less scrolling? More reading, more learning, more drawing. Less junk food? More fruit, more water. Less gossip? More honest talk, more silence, more self-reflection. An empty space will always get filled. Make sure you choose what fills it.

29. Make Promises You Can Keep

Do not make big promises you cannot keep. "I will never eat this again." "I will wake up at 4 am every day." "I will study 10 hours daily." When you break these big promises, you lose trust in yourself. Instead, make small, realistic promises. Keep them again and again until you believe your own words.

_____

_____

_____

_____

_____

_____

30. The Boring Part

Self-transformation is not always exciting. Many days are simple, even boring: Same time to wake, same exercise, same study time, same healthy meals. Boring is not bad. Boring is the sound of a strong life being built brick by brick.

31. One Thing at a Time

Trying to fix everything at once will break you. Choose one main habit to train first. Maybe: sleep, or study, or exercise, or controlling anger. Focus on that for some weeks until it becomes more natural. Then, add the next. Slow layers of discipline build a stable you.

_____

_____

_____

_____

_____

_____

32. When You Break the Chain

You were doing well. Days of discipline. Then one day you slip. You skip exercise. You binge watch. You waste hours on your phone. Do not say, "It's over. I failed. Why start again?" Say instead, "I broke the chain for one day. I will not let it become two, three, four." Get back on your path as soon as you notice you left it.

33. Your Environment Matters

Look around you. Is your room a mess? Is your desk full of distractions? Are your friends always pushing you towards trouble? Discipline is harder in a dirty, chaotic, negative space. Clean a little. Organize a little. Spend more time with people who also want to grow. Your environment should support your new self, not drag it down.

34. Learn to Delay

Self-mastery is the art of waiting. You see food, you wait a few minutes. You want to buy, you wait a few days. You feel anger, you wait before speaking. This small wait gives your brain time to think, "Is this good for me? Is this wise? Will this help my future?" Delay turns reactions into decisions.

35. The Power of "Just Today"

Thinking "I must be disciplined forever" can be heavy. So try this: "Just today, I will do what I said." Just today, I will study. Just today, I will control my temper. Just today, I will not watch mindless videos. Then, the next morning, say it again. A strong life is built from many strong "todays."

36. Track Your Effort

Want to feel your progress? Track it. Put a small mark on a calendar for every day you keep a habit. A tick for study. A tick for exercise. A tick for waking up on time. Soon you will see a line of marks that says, "I am changing, even if I don't feel it every day."

37. Discipline and Kindness

Discipline is not hating yourself. You do not shout, "I am useless, I am trash," to push yourself. That pain may make you move for a short time, but it breaks you in the end. Use firm kindness. "I am better than this. I know I can improve. I will not allow myself to stay weak, because I care about myself."

38. Don't Show Off the Grind

You do not have to show everyone your hard work. You do not need to post every study hour, every workout, every achievement. Let your results speak quietly for you later. Real discipline does not brag. It just works.

39. Rest With Intention

Self-mastery is not working nonstop. It is working with focus, then resting with purpose. Rest is not running away from your duties. Rest is charging your mind, your body, your heart, so you can come back stronger. Plan your rest like you plan your work.

_____

_____

_____

_____

_____

_____

40. Becoming Reliable to Yourself

The deepest power of discipline is this: You become someone you can rely on. When you say, "I will do it," you know you will. You do not wait for others to save you, push you, force you. You become the one who shows up for you every day. This is true self-mastery

CHAPTER 3 – MIND: MASTERING THOUGHTS AND EMOTIONS

41. The Mind Is Your Main Battlefield

Your real fight is not outside. Not with teachers, parents, friends, society. Your main fight is in your mind. Between the voice that says, "I can change," and the voice that says, "I will always be like this." Self-mastery is winning that inner battle again and again, thought by thought.

42. Watching Your Thoughts

Most days, thoughts run through your head like a wild river. You believe every thought: "I am ugly." "I am dumb." "No one cares." "It's hopeless." Try something new: Watch your thoughts like clouds in the sky. You see them, but you do not become them. You can say, "This is just a thought, not a fact."

_____

_____

_____

_____

_____

_____

43. Breaking the "Always" Spell

The words "always" and "never" are heavy chains. "I always fail." "I am always sad." "I will never change." "No one ever understands me." These words lock your mind in a dark room. Break the spell. Say instead, "I have failed before, but I can succeed too." "I feel sad now, but I have also smiled." "I struggled to change, but I can try again." Leave room for a new story.

44. Don't Believe Every Thought

Not every thought in your head is wise. Some thoughts are old fears, old insults, old pain repeating itself. When a thought comes, ask, "Is this helpful? Is this kind? Is this true?" If the answer is no, you can let it go like smoke from a fire that is not yours.

45. The Fear Voice

Fear has a voice. It says, "Don't try. You will embarrass yourself." "Don't speak. People will laugh." "Don't dream big. You'll get hurt." Fear's job is to keep you safe, but it often keeps you small. Listen, thank it for trying to protect you, then say, "I hear you, but I will still take one step."

46. From Overthinking to Action

Overthinking is like running on a treadmill. Your mind moves fast, but your life stays in the same place. "What if I fail? What if they judge? What if it goes wrong?" Ask yourself one more question: "What if I just try and see?" One small action can cut through a hundred scary thoughts.

47. Talking to Yourself Like a Friend

Listen to how you talk to yourself. "You're so stupid." "You can't do anything right." "Look at you, a mess." Would you say this to a friend who is struggling? Then do not say it to yourself. Change your tone: "I made a mistake, but I can learn." "I messed up, but I'm not trash." "I'm not okay now, but I'm working on it." This is how healing begins in the mind.

48. Breaking the "I Don't Care" Mask

"I don't care" is often a mask. You say it when you care too much and you are scared to show it. "I don't care about marks." "I don't care about my health." "I don't care about anyone." Deep inside, you do care. Self-mastery is taking off that mask and saying, "I care, and because I care, I will change how I live."

49. Turning Pain Into Power

Your mind remembers every hurt. Rejection, insults, broken trust, failure. You can let that pain turn into poison, telling you, "Don't try again. You are not worth it." Or you can say, "I will use this pain as fuel." "I will study harder." "I will train stronger." "I will become kinder, wiser, more focused." Pain can break you, or it can build you. You choose.

50. The Pause Button

A fast mind can destroy a peaceful life. You feel anger, you explode. You feel hurt, you attack. You feel fear, you run away. Self-mastery is learning to press a pause button. Three deep breaths. Count to ten. Walk away for a minute. In that tiny pause, you can choose a better response.

---

51. Healing Starts With "It Hurt"

Many of us try to be strong by saying, "It didn't hurt. I don't care. I'm fine." But the mind cannot heal what you refuse to admit. Say it softly: "It did hurt." "It did scare me." "It did make me feel small." This is not a weakness. This is step one of healing. You name the wound before you clean it.

52. Forgiving Yourself

Your mind can be a prison for old mistakes. "I shouldn't have done that." "I ruined everything." "I cannot forgive myself." But if you stay in that prison, you cannot grow. Look at your younger self with gentle eyes. "I did wrong, yes. I was not wise, yes. But I was learning. I am still learning. I will do better now." Forgiving yourself does not erase the past. It frees your hands to build a better future.

53. The Power of New Input

Your mind becomes what you feed it. If you feed it only drama, gossip, negativity, you will think in those colors. Start feeding it better things: Books that teach. Talks that inspire. Conversations that grow you. Music that lifts you. Bit by bit, your inner world changes shape.

54. Question Your Old Beliefs

Maybe you believe, "People always leave." "Everyone will hurt me." "I am not meant for success." Where did these beliefs come from? One bad event?

One person's words? Childhood pain? Ask, "Is this true for 100% of life? Or was it just true for that moment?" Breaking old beliefs is how you create room for becoming new.

55. Choosing Your Focus

What you focus on grows in your mind. If you only look at what you lack—money, looks, marks, love— you will feel empty. Try also to see what you do have: Any small skill. Any small progress. Any small support. Any small joy. This is not pretending everything is perfect. It is training your mind to see both pain and possibility.

56. Turning Jealousy Into Inspiration

You see others doing well and your mind says, "Why not me?" "They are better." "I hate them." Jealousy burns you from inside. Shift it: "That person shows what is possible.If they can do it, maybe I can too." Ask, "What can I learn from them?" Let other people's success push you forward, not pull you down.

57. Giving Your Emotions a Place

Your emotions need space, not a cage. When you lock them in, they show up later as anger, anxiety, or sudden tears. Find safe ways to express them: Write in a journal. Talk to a trusted person. Cry alone in your room. Create art, music, words. Let your emotions pass through, not pile up.

58. From "Why Me?" to "What Now?"

When something bad happens, your mind cries, "Why me?" "I did nothing to deserve this." This question keeps you stuck. Change it to, "What now?" "What can I do with this pain?" "What can I learn?" "How can I grow?" You cannot always choose what happens, but you can choose your next move.

59. Building a Calm Corner

Create a calm corner inside your mind. A place you can visit when everything feels loud. Maybe you remember a peaceful memory: a beach, a quiet room, a tree, a sunset. Close your eyes. Breathe. Imagine that place in detail. You can return there anytime, anywhere. This is how you carry peace inside you.

60. Becoming the Observer

When anger rises, don't just be angry. Be the one who sees it. "I feel anger in my chest." "My thoughts are fast." "I want to shout." When sadness comes, don't just be the sadness. Notice it. "I feel heavy." "My energy is low." "I want to hide." By observing, you create space between you and your emotions. In that space, you can choose what to do.

61. Accepting What You Cannot Control

Your mind gets tired trying to control things it can't: Other people's opinions. The past. The full future. Random events. Self-mastery is knowing where to stop. You say, "I will do my best with what I can change, and I will let go of what I cannot." This acceptance brings deep peace.

62. Training Mental Muscles

Just like your body, your mind has muscles. Focus, patience, positive thinking, self-control. Do not expect them to be strong without training. When you sit to study despite boredom, you train your focus. When you wait calmly instead of exploding, you train patience. When you look for solutions, not only problems, you train positive thinking. Keep training. Your mental muscles will grow.

_____

_____

_____

_____

_____

_____

63. Don't Live Only in Your Head

Thinking is good, but living only in your head can trap you. You plan, dream, worry, imagine, but you do not act. Remember you have a body and a life outside your thoughts. Talk to someone. Touch the ground. Do a small task. Move. Action pulls you back into reality and out of endless mental loops.

64. Healing the Inner Child

Inside you is a younger you who still hurts. The child who wasn't heard. The teen who was mocked. The small you who felt alone. Self-mastery includes healing that child. Imagine holding them. Tell them, "It was not your fault. You did your best. You were worthy all along. I am grown now. I will protect you. I will take care of us." This is how you become your own healer.

_____

_____

_____

_____

_____

_____

65. Writing Your New Script

Your mind has been acting from an old script. "Be quiet." "Don't dream." "Stay small." "Don't trust." You are allowed to write a new script: "I can speak with respect." "I can dream and also work." "I can take up space." "I can trust slowly and wisely." Repeat your new lines every day until your life begins to follow them.

66. The Quiet Rewire

Real change in the mind is often quiet. No big moments, no loud shouting, no dramatic scenes. Just many tiny choices like: "I won't insult myself today." "I will take three deep breaths before reacting." "I will focus for ten more minutes." Slowly, your brain rewires. You wake up one day and realize: "I don't think like I used to."

67. Becoming the Strong Mind

A strong mind is not one that never breaks. It is one that knows how to return to balance. You may still get angry, sad, jealous, afraid. But you know how to: Breathe. Question the thought. Choose a better action. Ask for help. Rest. Try again. That is strength: not perfect control, but steady recovery.

68. Letting Yourself Become New

Sometimes you are so used to your old mind that you are scared of the new one. Who am I if I am not always angry? Who am I if I am not the "funny, careless" one? Who am I if I start taking myself seriously? You are becoming someone you have not met yet. Allow it. Do not run back to the old cage just because it feels familiar.

69. Your Mind as a Garden

Think of your mind as a garden. Negative thoughts are weeds. Positive, true thoughts are flowers and strong trees. You cannot stop every weed from appearing, but you can pull them out when you see them, and plant better seeds. "I am learning." "I can change." "I am worthy of respect." "I am building a better me." Water these thoughts daily. Watch your inner world bloom.

70. The Master From Within

True self-mastery is not about controlling everything. It is about knowing yourself deeply and leading yourself gently but firmly. You are not waiting for someone to save your mind, to calm your heart, to discipline your habits. You are slowly becoming the master from within: Aware. Honest. Patient. Focused. Always learning. This is the beginning of a new you from the inside out.

_____

_____

_____

_____

_____

_____

CHAPTER 4 – BREAKING & HEALING: LETTING GO AND RISING AGAIN

71. When Your Old Self Breaks

There comes a time when your old self cannot carry you anymore. The lazy you. The angry you. The scared you. The careless you. You try to live like before, but something inside starts breaking. Do not panic. This breaking is not the end. It is your old skin cracking so a new you can breathe.

72. The Hurt You Don't Show

You smile. You joke. You say, "I'm fine." But inside, there are cuts no one sees. Words they threw at you. Love that left. Dreams that failed. You don't have to show this hurt to everyone, but you must show it to yourself. See it. Name it. Admit it. What you hide cannot heal.

73. Breaking the Old Patterns

Notice what keeps repeating in your life. Same kind of fights. Same kind of friends. Same late nights. Same regrets. These are patterns. Breaking them is not about one big act. It is about changing one step in the old dance. You pause before you shout. You say no to that friend. You sleep one hour earlier. Change one move. The whole pattern will slowly fall apart.

74. It's Okay to Fall Apart

Sometimes you need to fall apart for a while. To cry hard. To feel tired. To admit, "I am not okay." Strong people also have days when they feel weak. Let yourself break a little in safe places— in your room, in your journal, with someone you trust. Broken does not mean finished. It means you are ready to be rebuilt.

75. Letting Go of People

Some people belong only to one chapter of your story, not the whole book. Friends who pull you down. Lovers who disrespect you. Groups that push you towards trouble. Letting them go will hurt. You will miss what you had, even if it was not good for you. But you cannot heal in the same place that keeps wounding you.

76. Saying Goodbye to an Old Version

You are changing. But a part of you misses the old life. The late nights. The careless jokes. The easy comfort. The unhealthy fun. Write a goodbye to that old version: "Thank you for helping me survive when I knew no better. But now I am moving on. I need to grow, even if it hurts. I release you with love." This is not hate. It is a peaceful break.

77. The Pain of Healing

Healing is not soft all the time. Sometimes it burns. Like cleaning a deep wound. Like moving a bone back into place. You remember old memories. You face hard truths. You forgive people who never said sorry. Do not stop just because it hurts. This pain is fixing what broken pain created.

78. Allowing Yourself to Grieve

You can grieve many things: A person. A dream. A certain age. A version of yourself. Grief is love looking for a home that is no longer there. Do not rush it. Do not say, "I should be over this by now." Cry. Talk. Write. Pray. Sit in silence. Every tear is a step toward release.

79. Not All Breaking Is Failure

We think breaking means we failed. But sometimes breaking means we grow. The old shell of a seed must crack for a plant to come out. The old limits must snap for a bigger life to begin. If your old ways can no longer hold you, it is a sign you are ready for more.

80. The Courage to Ask for Help

Healing alone is heavy. You are brave, but you are human. There is no shame in saying, "I need someone to listen." "I need advice." "I need support." A friend, a mentor, a counselor, a family member, someone you trust. Asking for help does not make you weak. It means you are serious about healing.

81. Turning Shame Into Understanding

Shame whispers, "If people knew what you did, if people knew what happened to you, they would hate you." So you hide. But in hiding, you hit yourself again and again with the same memory. Slowly tell yourself, "I did not know better back then. I was younger. I was hurt. I was confused. Now I choose different." Understanding softens shame so healing can enter.

82. You Don't Have to Stay Broken

Some people start to wear their pain as an identity. "I am broken. I am damaged. I am ruined." They believe this is who they must be forever. You don't. You can say, "I have been broken, yes. But I am also healing. Learning. Becoming. My pain is a part of me, not all of me."

83. Gentle With Your Scars

Scars are proof that something once hurt you deeply, but now it is closed. You may still feel a small ache. You may still remember. Be gentle with your scars. Touch them with respect, not hate. They are signs that you did not give up when it hurt the most.

84. Rewriting the Memory

You cannot erase the past, but you can rewrite the meaning of it. Instead of, "That breakup proved I am worthless," say, "That breakup showed me what love is NOT." Instead of, "That failure proved I am stupid," say, "That failure taught me how not to do it." You are not changing what happened, you are changing what it means to your story.

85. Slow Healing Is Still Healing

You want to be "over it" fast. No more tears. No more triggers. No more hard days. But some wounds are deep. They heal slowly, layer by layer. One day you still cry. Another day you feel fine. This is normal. Do not judge your pace. Slow healing is still healing.

86. Breaking the Need to Be Perfect

Sometimes your healing gets blocked by your need to be perfect. You think, "If I make one mistake, I am back to zero." This is not true. You can heal and still have bad days. You can grow and still mess up. Perfection breaks. Progress bends but does not snap. Choose progress.

_____

_____

_____

_____

_____

_____

87. Closing Old Doors

There are doors in your life you must close to move on. Old chats you keep reading. Old photos you keep checking. Old groups you keep re-entering, hoping they changed. Closing the door will hurt. You will feel empty for a while. But you cannot enter a new room while you keep one foot in the old one.

88. Forgiving Others for Yourself

Some people may never say, "I'm sorry." They will act like they did nothing wrong. If you wait for their apology to heal, you give them too much power. Forgiveness does not mean what they did was okay. It means you will not let their actions control your heart anymore. You forgive so you can be free.

89. When You Are Angry at Life

Sometimes you are not just hurt— you are angry at life itself. "Why me? Why this? Why now?" Let yourself feel that anger. Talk it out. Write it out. Then, gently, tell life: "I don't understand why this happened. But I will not let it turn me bitter. I will turn this fire into light if I can."

90. Tiny Acts of Self-Care

Healing does not happen only in big talks or heavy tears. It also lives in small acts of self-care: Taking a shower when you feel numb. Eating a proper meal. Opening your window to let light in. Changing your bedsheet. Stretching your body. These tiny actions send a message to your soul: "I still care about you."

_____

_____

_____

_____

_____

_____

91. Letting Your Heart Open Again

After being hurt, your heart wants to close. "No more friends. No more love. No more trust." Closing feels safe, but it also blocks joy. You do not have to open your heart all at once. Open it like a door with a chain. A little. Look. Listen. Check. Let good people prove they are safe over time.

92. Healing While Still Hurting

You may think, "I must feel fully okay before I can build my life again." But healing often happens while you are still hurting. You go to class with a heavy heart. You work with wet eyes. You practice self-control even while you feel rage. This is not fake. This is strength. You are learning to move with your pain, not wait until it vanishes.

93. The Moment You Choose to Live

There is a quiet moment in healing where you choose: "I will live fully, even if I have scars. I will love again. I will try again. I will dream again. My story did not end in that dark chapter." That choice may not erase the sadness, but it turns you towards the light.

94. Trusting the Process

Healing is not a straight line. It is a messy road with turns, stops, and surprise drops. You may think, "I am back where I started." But look closely: Your reactions are softer. Your awareness is stronger. Your choices are wiser. Trust the process. Every honest step is part of your becoming.

95. Rising From Your Own Ashes

Like a phoenix in old stories, you also can burn down to almost nothing and still rise. Not as the same old self, but as a new one: More aware. More steady. More kind. More powerful. You are not only the fire that destroyed you. You are also the wings that grow after.

96. Healing as a Daily Practice

Healing is not one big event. It is a daily practice: Choosing not to text the one who hurt you. Choosing to rest instead of escape. Choosing to speak instead of explode. Choosing to be honest with yourself about how you feel. Every day you make these choices, you are slowly stitching your heart back together

CHAPTER 5 – BECOMING: RISING AS YOUR NEW SELF

97. The Space Between Who You Were and Who You Are

There is a strange space in transformation. You are no longer your old self, but not yet your full new self. You feel in-between, unsteady, confused. This is normal. Becoming is a bridge, not a jump. Walk it slowly. Step by step, you will feel more at home in the new you.

98. Choosing Your Next Version

You are not a random result. You can choose the kind of person you want to become. Honest? Disciplined? Calm? Brave? Kind? Focused? Write it down: "My next version is a person who..." Then ask each day, "What would that person do in this situation?" And do it, even if it feels new and strange.

_____

_____

_____

_____

_____

_____

99. Living by Your Own Values

Becoming new is not about pleasing everyone. It is about knowing what you stand for. Respect. Hard work. Loyalty. Truth. Health. Faith. Whatever your values are, live by them, even when no one is watching. That is how you build a strong core inside.

100. Building a New Identity

Instead of saying, "I am trying to be disciplined," say, "I am a disciplined person who trains daily." Instead of, "I am trying to be healthy," say, "I am a person who cares for their body." Identity drives action. When you decide who you are, your choices slowly begin to match it.

101. Keeping Your Standards

Your new self has standards. How people can talk to you. How you talk to others. What behavior you accept from yourself. When someone crosses those lines, speak up or step back. When you yourself cross them, admit it and correct it. Standards protect your becoming.

102. The Power of Small Wins

Your new self is built on small wins, not only big ones. You woke up on time. Win. You controlled your temper. Win. You studied when you wanted to procrastinate. Win. Collect these wins like coins in a jar. One day you will look back and realize you are rich in self-respect.

_____

_____

_____

_____

_____

_____

103. Handling People Who Knew the Old You

Some people will only remember the old you. The one who joked too much, never cared, never tried. They may say, "You've changed," like it's a bad thing. Smile and say, "Yes, I have." You do not need everyone's permission to grow. In time, those who matter will adjust to your new level— or fall away.

104. Practicing Until It Feels Natural

At first, your new habits and new reactions will feel fake. You will think, "This is not me." But the truth is, this is you in training. Like learning a new language, it feels strange in the beginning. Keep practicing. One day you will respond with calm, with discipline, with wisdom— and only later realize, "This used to be so hard for me."

_____

_____

_____

_____

_____

_____

105. Carrying Yourself Differently

Becoming new shows in small details. You sit with more presence. You walk with more purpose. You look people in the eye. You listen without needing to impress. This is not arrogance. It is the quiet confidence of someone who knows they are working on themselves.

106. Saying "No" Without Guilt

The new you must learn the power of "no." No to bad habits. No to toxic people. No to overcommitting. No to anything that pulls you away from your path. You can say "no" calmly, without anger, without guilt. Every "no" to what harms you is a "yes" to who you are becoming.

_____

_____

_____

_____

_____

_____

107. Letting Your Actions Speak

You don't need to keep telling people, "I've changed." Let your actions speak: Your consistency. Your calm reactions. Your respect. Your work. Quiet growth is powerful. Those who are watching will notice, slowly, surely.

108. Becoming a Person You Respect

You want respect from others. But first, become someone you respect yourself. When you look in the mirror, can you say, "I am trying honestly. I am not cheating myself. I am living closer to my values each day." Self-respect is the foundation of real confidence.

109. Choosing Long-Term Over Short-Term

Old you wanted comfort now. New you chose strength later. Watch how you decide: More sleep vs. keeping your promise. More junk vs. caring for your body. More gossip vs. protecting your peace. Every time you choose long-term gain over short-term pleasure, you step deeper into the new you.

110. The Friends of Your Future

Ask yourself, "Does this person fit in the future I am building?" Do they support your growth? Respect your change? Challenge you to be better? Or do they mock your efforts, pull you back, keep you stuck in old patterns? Becoming new sometimes means finding new circles that match your new level.

111. Becoming Reliable to Others

Self-mastery is not only for yourself. As you grow, you become more reliable for others too. If you say you will be there, you are. If you say you will help, you do. People start to trust your word. Your transformation becomes a blessing for more than just you.

112. Staying Humble While You Rise

As you improve, pride may try to enter. "I am better than them." "I know more." "I work harder. They are lazy." Be careful. You were once where they are. You still have much to learn. Stay humble: Strong, but not harsh. Confident, but not cruel. Real masters do not look down. They lift others up.

_____

_____

_____

_____

_____

_____

113. Creating New Traditions for Yourself

Create small personal traditions that support your becoming. A weekly check-in with yourself. A monthly goal review. A morning routine. An evening reflection. These rituals anchor your new self in daily life. They remind you, "This is who I am now. This is how I live."

114. The Quiet Joy of Growth

There is a special joy that comes when you notice your own growth. You stayed calm where you once exploded. You kept going where you once gave up. You spoke the truth where you once lied. No one else may see it, but you do. Smile. Celebrate. This quiet joy is the reward of becoming.

_____

_____

_____

_____

_____

_____

115. Holding On When It Feels Pointless

Some days you will wonder, "Why am I even doing all this? No one sees. Nothing big changed yet." Remember: Seeds look pointless in the soil for a long time. Then suddenly, they break through. Your efforts are under the surface right now. Keep going. Your time of visible growth will come.

116. Mixing Strength With Softness

The new you is not hard all the time. Strength without softness closes your heart. Becoming whole means you can be: Firm with your boundaries, yet gentle with people. Disciplined with your habits, yet kind to yourself. Strong in your decisions, yet open to learning. This balance is true maturity.

117. Teaching Others by Example

You don't have to preach to inspire. Just live your transformation honestly. Your younger siblings, friends, or even strangers may see you and think, "If they can change, maybe I can too." You become a living lesson that growth is possible.

118. Accepting That Not Everyone Will Understand

Some will say, "You act different." "Why so serious now?" "You've changed, you're boring." Smile softly. They are looking at you through old eyes. You are not living to fit their idea of you. You are living to become who you were meant to be. Understanding is a gift, not a requirement.

_____

_____

_____

_____

_____

_____

119. Checking In With Your Old Triggers

Meet your old triggers from your new place. The person who used to make you angry. The topic that made you feel small. The situation that made you run away. Notice how you respond now. Maybe still shaky, but a little more in control. This is proof: you are not the same person anymore.

120. Becoming a Work in Progress Forever

You may think one day you will be "finished." No more doubts. No more mistakes. No more struggle. But real masters never stop being students. You will always have more to learn, more to refine, more to understand. This is not sad. It means you get to keep becoming for your whole life

CHAPTER 6 – FALLING & RISING: STAYING ON THE PATH WHEN YOU SLIP

121. Slipping Is Part of the Journey

You will slip. You will miss days. You will lose your temper. You will return to old habits. This does not mean you are a failure. It means you are human and learning. Self-mastery is not about never slipping. It is about how quickly and how wisely you rise.

122. The First Mistake vs. The Second

The first mistake is human. You ate junk. You didn't study. You skipped exercise. The danger is the second mistake: "I already messed up, so it doesn't matter now." It does matter. Stop the fall at one mistake. Do not turn one wrong step into a whole wrong road.

_____

_____

_____

_____

_____

_____

123. Don't Throw Away the Whole Day

You break one habit in the morning and say, "Today is ruined." So you stop trying, and really do ruin the day. Instead, say, "Only this moment went wrong. The rest of the day is still in my hands." Salvage what you can. One bad minute does not have to become a bad day.

124. Owning Your Slip

When you fall, do not hide behind excuses. "I was tired." "My friends made me." "It just happened." Say instead, "I chose this. I knew better. I slipped." It may feel heavy, but this honesty gives you power. What you own, you can change.

125. Talk to Yourself After You Fall

After a slip, your mind may shout, "You're useless. See? You can't change."
Do not let that be the last word. Answer yourself: "Yes, I fell. But I am still
on this path. I will stand up, adjust, and continue." You are not your worst
moment. You are what you do after it.

126. Learning From the Fall

Every fall carries a lesson. Ask, "What was I feeling right before?" "Who was
I with?" "What triggered me?" "What can I change next time?" Maybe you
were hungry, tired, lonely, bored. Adjust your life around those weak
moments. Turn each fall into a teacher.

_____

_____

_____

_____

_____

_____

127. The Shame Spiral

Shame says, "You fell. Now hide. Don't tell anyone. Don't try again." So you stay alone with your mistake, and the weight grows. Break the spiral: Share with someone you trust. Write it down. Face it in the open. Light shrinks shame.

128. Rest Is Not Quitting

Sometimes you don't need more pushing. You need rest. Your body is tired. Your mind is overloaded. Your heart is heavy. Resting wisely for a while— sleep, quiet time, simple joy— is not quitting. It is recharging so you can return stronger.

129. Resetting the Next Morning

No matter how badly you fell today, morning is a reset button. Wake up, wash your face, breathe deep, and say, "New day. New choices. I return to my path." Do not carry yesterday's dirt into today's sunrise.

130. When Old Environments Pull You Back

You visit old places, old groups, old routines, and suddenly the old you wakes up. You slip into the same jokes, same habits, same choices. Notice it. You may need new spaces, new routes, new company until your new self is strong enough to stand anywhere.

_____

_____

_____

_____

_____

_____

131. The "What's the Point?" Trap

After failing a few times, you may think, "What's the point? I'll always be like this." This thought is a trap. You are judging your whole future by a few past days. See your progress as a long road, not a single step. The point is not perfection. The point is direction.

132. Comparing Your Falls With Others' Success

On your low days, everyone else will look perfect. Their marks, their body, their confidence, their life. You compare your worst moment with their best photo. Stop. You do not see their hidden falls. You only see your own. Focus back on your lane. Rise for yourself.

133. Allowing Yourself to Be a Beginner Again

When you fall hard, you may need to start small again. Less weight. Shorter study times. Simpler goals. Your ego will say, "But I was doing so much more before." Ignore it. Better to start as a humble beginner than to quit as a proud failure.

134. Keeping One Anchor Habit

In storms, anchors keep ships from drifting away. Choose one simple habit as your anchor when life is messy. Maybe: making your bed, or a short prayer, or ten minutes of reading, or a walk. Even when everything falls apart, keep that one habit. It will remind you: "I am still that person who is trying."

_____

_____

_____

_____

_____

_____

135. The Power of Returning

The real magic word in transformation is not "start." It is "return." Return after failure. Return after sadness. Return after numb days. Every time you return to your path, you prove to yourself that your decision to grow is real.

136. Apologizing and Repairing

When your fall hurts others, rising again includes repair. Say, "I was wrong." "I am sorry." "I am working on myself." You cannot force them to forgive, but you can show through time and action that you are serious about change. This is also self-mastery.

137. Laughing at Yourself Kindly

Sometimes you will overreact, act foolish, and repeat an old habit in a funny way. Instead of hating yourself, learn to smile and say, "There I go again, being human." Kind laughter releases tension and keeps you light while you grow.

138. Remembering How Far You've Come

On bad days, your mind only sees your current failure. Pause and look back. Remember where you started. What you used to do. How you used to think. List the changes, even if they're small. You are not where you want to be, but you are also not where you were. Honor that distance.

139. Keeping Your Vision in Front of You

When you fall, lift your eyes back to your vision. The person you want to become. The life you are building. The peace you are seeking. Write it on paper. Put it on your wall. Keep it on your phone. Let your future call you forward whenever your past pulls you back.

140. Rising Gently, Rising Strong

After a hard fall, don't jump up too fast to prove you are okay. Rise gently. Breathe. Reflect. Adjust your plan. Then rise strong. Take one clear step. Then another. Every time you rise, you become a little more unbreakable.

CHAPTER 7 – LIVING IN SELF-MASTERY: DAILY LIFE OF THE NEW YOU

141. A Normal Day in a Strong Life

Self-masterydoes not always lookdramatic.It looks like a normal daylived with intention.You wake with purpose.You do your work with focus.You rest without guilt.You speak with respect.Nothing "viral,"nothing loud—just a steady life built on strong choices.

142. Morning: Meeting Yourself First

Before you meet the world,meet yourself.A few minutes of quiet.A short prayer,affirmation,or reflection.A planfor your main tasks.You tell the day,"I will lead you,not be dragged by you."This is how self-mastery starts every morning.

_____

_____

_____

_____

_____

_____

143. Setting Daily Intentions

Each day,choosea simple focus."TodayI practice patience." "Today I give my best to my work." "Today I protect my peace." During the day,check: "Am I living my intention?" Small daily intentions shape a powerful life.

144. Moving With Awareness

Walk,sit,work,and speakwith awareness.Not rushed,not half-awake.Notice your breath.Notice your posture.Notice your tone.You are not justa bodyrushing around.You are a conscious beingchoosing howto movethrough your day

145. Mastery in Ordinary Tasks

Self-mastery shows up in simple tasks: Washing dishes properly. Finishing homework on time.Answering messages with respect. Doing your job even when no one is watching. How you do small thingsis how you trainfor big things.

146. Guarding Your Mental Space

You decidewhat entersyour mind. You cannot stop every thought, but you can reduce what feeds them. Limit useless arguments, constant news, toxic pages, endless gossip. Choose what strengthens you.Your mind is precious space—protect it.

147. Eating and Sleeping Like You Matter

A mastered life includes a cared-for body.You try to eat food that gives energy,not just comfort.You aim for enough sleep so your brain can function well.Not perfect,but conscious.Your habits say,"I treat myself like someone who matters."

148. Speaking With Intention

Before you speak, you ask yourself: "Is it true?" "Is it kind?" "Is it necessary?" You avoid useless criticism, pointless arguments, and cheap gossip. Your words carry weight,because you don't throw them carelessly.

149. Handling Conflict Calmly

In self-mastery, conflict does not disappear, but you meet it differently. You listen before reacting. You state your side without shouting. You walk away when it's just ego fighting ego. You choose peace over winning, truth over drama.

150. Using Technology, Not Being Used by It

Your phone,your apps,your gamesare tools—not your masters.You decide when to be online,when to reply,when to stop.You create borders: No phone during deep work.No endless scrolling right before sleep.You use tech to grow,not to escape.

_____

_____

_____

_____

_____

_____

151. Building Meaningful Connections

The new you values depth over just numbers. You may not have hundreds of close people, but you build a few safe, honest connections. You listen. You show up. You speak truth

152. The Quiet Turning

Self-mastery is not a trumpet blast. It is the quiet turning of your face toward the truth again, and again, and again.

_____

_____

_____

_____

_____

_____

153. The Small Steering Wheel

You cannot calm the storm, but you can loosen your fingers from the wheel of panic, and place them, gently, on the small steering wheel of your own response.This is all you ever own. This is more than enough.

154. Discipline as Devotion

Discipline is not a cage. It is the path you draw through the wild grass to visit the future you say you want every single day.

155. The Inner Room

In every person there is a room no one else can enter. Self-mastery is learning to sit there, to clean the dust, to open a window, to light a lamp and not be afraid of the furniture you find.

156. Your Hands on the Clay

Your life is wet clay. The world pushes, pulls, leaves its fingerprints. Self-mastery is the moment your own hands press back, not to erase but to shape.

157. The Second Thought

You may not rule your first thought, that flash of fear, that spark of anger. But the second thought, the one that chooses what to do with the first— that one is yours. Guard it. Train it. Trust it.

158. Fire and Hearth

You were born with wildfire in you. Self-mastery is not killing the flames, it is learning how to build a hearth so your fire can warm instead of burn.

_____

_____

_____

_____

_____

_____

159. Owning Your Name

No voice outside you gets to name you without your consent. Self-mastery is when you learn to say softly, but completely: "This is who I am," and then walk in that direction even when no one claps.

160. The Practice of Returning

You will drift. You will forget. You will be pulled by every loud desire. Self-mastery is not a straight line. It is the practice of returning to what matters, gently, like bringing a child back home.

161. The Mirror Without Hate

Stand before the mirror without weapon words. Self-mastery is looking at your own face without trying to win or lose, only to see, and from that seeing, to choose.

162. The Unsentences

There are words you do not send. Replies you do not post. Self-mastery is the quiet stack of unsent sentences that proves you are no longer willing to be dragged by every passing storm.

163. The Long Game

Pleasure calls from the corner. Purpose waits at the horizon. Self-mastery is the art of hearing both voices and still choosing the road your future self will thank you for.

164. Meeting Your Shadow

You are not finished where you are flawless. You are finished where you are honest. Self-mastery is shaking hands with the parts of you you once tried to bury, and teaching them how to work for you, not against you.

165. The Still Point

Between impulse and action there is a still point. Self-mastery is learning to live there for one extra breath, long enough to turn reaction into choice.

166. Quiet Victories

No one sees the moment you get out of bed when it would be easier not to. No one applauds the thought you refuse to feed. Self-mastery is built of these invisible victories stacked, day upon day, until even you cannot deny the weight of them.

_____

_____

_____

_____

_____

_____

167. The Rope and the Climb

You are not your past. You are the rope you throw upward from it.
Self-mastery is blistered hands, refusing to let go even when the sky is still
out of reach.

168. Listening to Yourself

You ask everyone what you should do with your one small life. Self-mastery
is the day you realize the quietest voice in the room is the only one that has
lived inside your skin.

_____

_____

_____

_____

_____

_____

169. Training the Heart

Self-mastery is not only a sharp mind. It is a trained heart— one that can feel without drowning, that can care without collapsing, that can forgive without forgetting what it deserves.

170. The Unfinished Sculpture

You are a sculpture carving itself. Every promise kept, every habit dropped, every boundary drawn is one more strike of the chisel. Self-mastery is accepting you will never be finished, and carving anyway.

_____

_____

_____

_____

_____

_____

171. The Weight You Choose

You will carry something— regret or discipline, avoidance or courage.

Self-mastery is choosing the heavier weight now so you do not have to bow under the heavier one later.

172. The Lion on a Leash

Anger is a lion. So is desire. So is fear. Self-mastery does not cage the lion until it dies. It walks beside it with a strong leash, eyes open, ready to say: "Not today. Not this."

_____

_____

_____

_____

_____

_____

173. The Daily Promise

Self-mastery is not a vow you make once. It is the daily promise to be a little more honest, a little more present, a little more aligned with the person you keep seeing in your best imagination.

174. The Art of Letting Go

There are battles you win by walking away. Self-mastery is the courage to drop the rope when you realize you were only pulling against your own reflection.

_____

_____

_____

_____

_____

_____

175. Your Own Permission

You have waited for doors to open, for voices to invite you, for signs to appear. Self-mastery is understanding that the permission slip you needed was always supposed to be written in your own handwriting.

176. The Final Authority

At the end, when the noise has drained from the day, all that remains is you and the quiet question: "Did I rule myself today, or did I hand that power to everything that knocked?" Self-mastery is slowly learning to answer "Today, I chose me.

One Last Note

When you picked up this book, you made a quiet but powerful declaration: "I am willing to meet myself." That, more than any technique or idea, is the heart of self-mastery and self-transformation.

If there is one message I hope stays with you, it is this: you are not a finished product, you are an ongoing practice. Self-mastery is not a dramatic overnight change; it is a series of small, honest choices made in ordinary moments. It is how you speak to yourself when no one is listening, how you respond when things don't go your way, how you return to your values after you've drifted from them.

As you step beyond these pages, you will be tested—not by grand events, but by daily life. You will meet old patterns in new clothes. You will feel the pull of your past, the noise of other people's opinions, the seduction of comfort and distraction. This is not a sign that you have failed; it is proof that you are human. Self-mastery does not mean you never fall; it means you fall more consciously, rise more quickly, and learn more deeply each time.

Remember:

You always have a choice, even if it is a small one: one different thought, one slower breath, one kinder word, one aligned action.

Transformation is not about becoming someone else; it is about becoming fully, courageously yourself.

Discipline and compassion must walk together. Hold yourself to a higher standard, but do it with understanding, not hatred.

_____

_____

_____

_____

_____

_____

Progress is often invisible. Trust the quiet shifts: the arguments you avoid, the habits you no longer feed, the boundaries you now protect.

Take what has resonated with you from this book and turn it into your own living practice. Don't try to apply everything at once. Choose a few principles, one or two habits, and live them consistently. Let your life—not your memory of these pages—be the real classroom.

There will be days when you will forget what you've learned. On those days, return to the simplest truths: breathe, observe, be honest, and choose the next right step. Every time you come back to yourself, you are strengthening the very mastery you seek.

Thank you for allowing these words into your inner world, for your willingness to question, to feel, and to grow. My hope is that you close this book not with a sense of completion, but with a quiet, steady resolve:

_____

_____

_____

_____

_____

_____

To lead yourself before you seek to lead others.

To create inner order before you chase outer success.

To live in such a way that your daily actions reflect your deepest values.

Your life from this point forward is your true "last chapter." May you write it with awareness, courage, and compassion—for yourself and for everyone whose life your transformation will touch